A gift for: _____

From: _____

Laugh Lines

Getting Older, Getting Wiser, Getting It Right

by **LIZA DONNELLY**

GIFT BOOKS

CHRONICLE BOOKS
SAN FRANCISCO

For my daughters, Ella and Gretchen

Copyright © 2010 by Liza Donnelly.
All rights reserved. No part of this book may
be reproduced in any form without written
permission from the publisher.

Published in 2011 by Hallmark Gift Books,
a division of Hallmark Cards Inc.,
under license from Chronicle Books.

Visit us on the Web at www.hallmark.com.

DESIGNED BY Jennifer Tolo Pierce

ISBN: 978-1-59530-447-6
BOK2127
Printed and bound in China
JUL11

contents

CHAPTER 1 *page* 7

Growing Up

CHAPTER 2 *page* 27

20s

CHAPTER 3 *page* 45

30s

CHAPTER 4 *page* 63

40s

CHAPTER 5 *page* 87

50s

CHAPTER 6 *page* 107

60s and beyond

"I can't decide what I'm going to be when I grow up—a good girl or a slut."

CHAPTER 1

Growing Up

When do you know that you're a girl?

My mother did not invest a lot of money in pink. For one thing, I was her second daughter—and in the beginning, she was busy recuperating from my dangerously early arrival (three months premature!). As loving as she was, we did not do girly things like shopping or painting nails. The only other girl in the house—except for our dog, Sassy—was my rebellious sister, whose tactics incited fear and anger. I quickly learned to be the good girl. Amid these women, it became clear that someone had actually wanted a boy. My father took me to baseball games and taught me golf—all attention I loved. It became a running joke in the family.

At some point, I discovered drawing, and it has saved me.

I learned that being a girl was secondary to my concerns, and I positioned myself quietly on the outside of it all. My cartoons were my identity, and they did the talking/dressing/expressing for me. It has been quite a journey since.

Where it all begins:

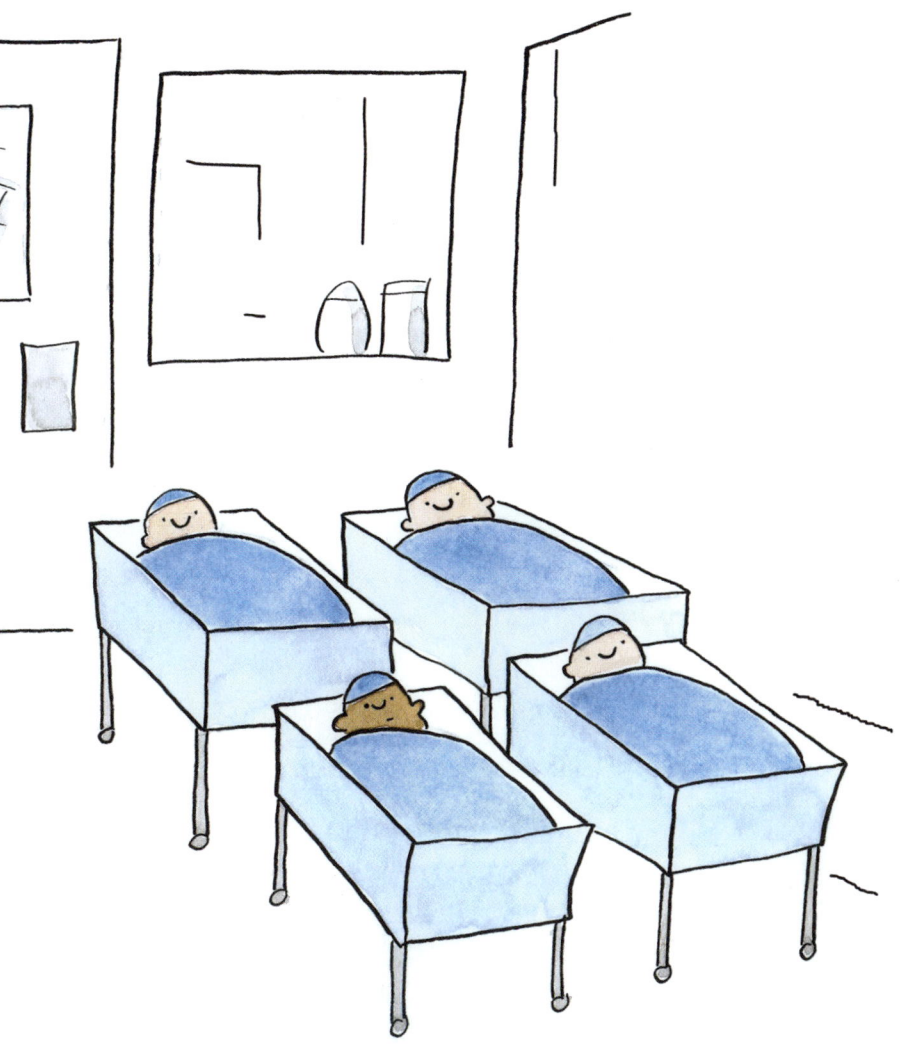

MOTHERS come in many versions

A. How to make granola
B. How to protest any and everything
C. How to question gender construction
D. the importance of makeup
E. How to be sweet in any situation
F. How to be brainy and sexy
G. How to get the job — whatever it is — done

TRYING on MOM'S STUFF

FEELINGS ABOUT BARBIE

YOUR PERIOD

NOT REALITY

REALITY

HAIRSTYLES to avoid IN HIGH SCHOOL

"Do you think my pink Miley Cyrus leggings go with my pink Lady Gaga backpack and my pink Beyoncé earrings? Should I be wearing my pink Britney Spears skirt with my pink Paris Hilton tank, you think?"

Prom Dresses to Forget

the First Kiss

made you want to throw up.

confused you.

hooked you.

made you wonder what hands have to do with a kiss.

What *is* sex?

"In one day, I went from tweeting my oatmeal to tweeting a revolution."

CHAPTER 2

20s

When I moved to New York City in 1977, I had really long blonde hair. I mean, down-below-my-waist long. I loved that my *hair* got attention—and it hid my curves, which I had grown to hate. I wore Earth shoes and refused to wear makeup, paint my nails, or read women's magazines. It was my rebellion of sorts. But it was also a cop-out. Since my hair said "female" in volumes, I did not have to acknowledge my womanness. But there came a time when I realized I had to cut it.

I had never been to a salon before. Clueless, I just picked one near my apartment. When I walked in, the stylist stared at me with a combination of utter disgust and glee, and showed me to the chair. What happened next was a blur. I had finally "come of age"—in a hair salon.

For the next 10 years, I cartooned and dated. I was finding my voice in what I created, how I looked, and who I was with. I tried to find that elusive middle ground—that perfect mix of smart, creative, ambitious (but not *too*), thoughtful, funny, attractive. I spoke very little, fearful my words would betray my lack of confidence. I dated a lot, and my career—while successful—lurched along. But nothing fit right—I found myself casting aside clothing, men, and cartoons on a weekly basis. It was as if this decade was a time to figure out what I *didn't* want.

One thing stayed the same: I never had long hair again.

LOOKING for a JOB?

What not to wear:

What not to say:

I'm not sure I'm very good.

I can really kick butt!

I've been thinking how your company needs help. It sucks.

what not to do:

kiss the interviewer.

Do your favorite dance.

what not to submit:

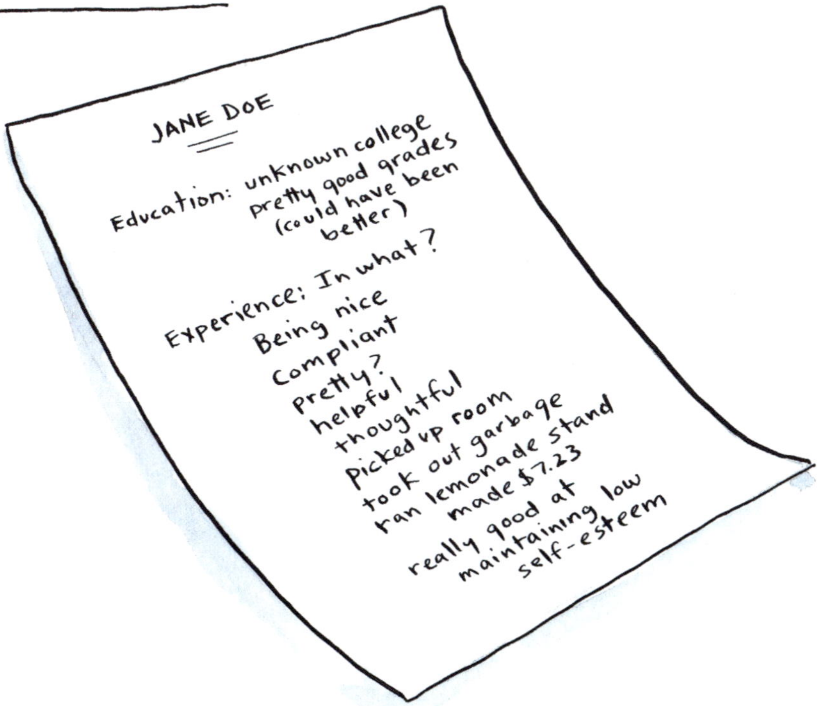

JANE DOE

Education: unknown college
pretty good grades
(could have been better)

Experience: In what?
Being nice
compliant
pretty?
helpful
thoughtful
picked up room
took out garbage
ran lemonade stand
made $7.23
really good at maintaining low self-esteem

HAIRSTYLES to AVOID in your 20s

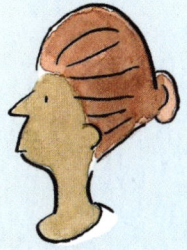

Mirror Talk

"Some of my best friends are married."

CHAPTER 3

30s

When I turned 30, I threw myself a party. I invited all my friends. I even took a chance and invited a man I had met recently, a fellow cartoonist for *The New Yorker*. As it turned out, he couldn't come.

Marriage had been on my mind. I had decided to accept the idea of marriage for myself. I had expected to get married by 28. It seemed reasonable. But there were a few problems. The men I dated were either noncommittal, incommunicative, wore strange clothing, chewed with their mouths open, or all of the above. And I was trying too hard to mold myself to them. It seemed I didn't know myself anymore, much less what I wanted. My shrink suggested—news flash—that maybe it had something to do with my parents' divorce. But like a good shrink, she offered no concrete prescription, so I kept on going.

Just when I thought I was destined to be the stereotypic lonely, pathetic, angry, man-hating, children-hating, cranky, frumpy, "eccentric" old maid, things changed. The man who couldn't come to my 30th birthday party entered my life four years later—and we got married. We had finally found each other. How did I know it was right? Maybe I needed to have all those boyfriends, or maybe those extra four years made the difference. Maybe it was simply the feeling that I was myself again.

HAIRSTYLES to AVOID in your 30s

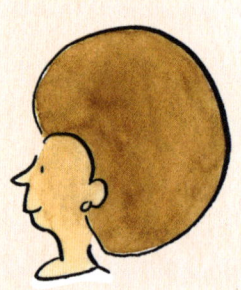

What we wish construction workers would really say:

a. You look really intelligent!
b. You chose some great color combinations!
c. You look like an important person!
d. They're going to promote you today!
e. You don't look old!
f. We're idiots and apologize for man's insensitivity to women.

If you look like this in your 30s people will assume...

- You are a lesbian
- You are a Fran Lebowitz wannabe
- You are attempting to climb the corporate ladder without resorting to using your sex
- You were a women's studies major

So you've got work figured out — good job, steady pay, room for advancement. You put off settling down for this and it's paid off.

THEN...

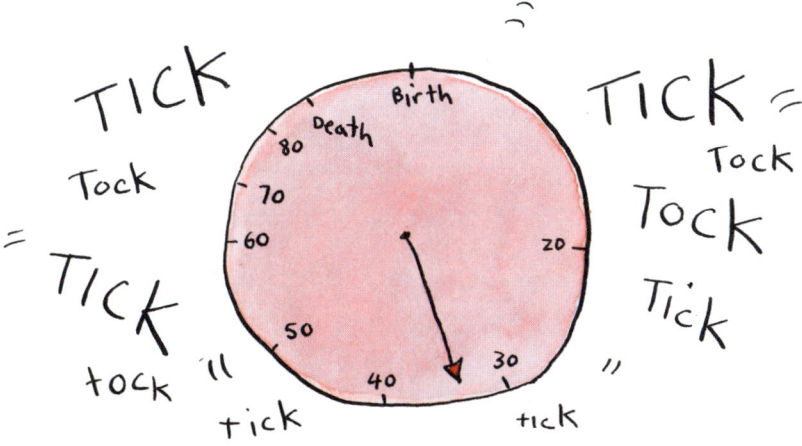

The biological clock gets REALLY LOUD!

DO YOU REALLY WANT KIDS?

they're messy

they're noisy

they're expensive

they're needy

they're funny

they love unconditionally

"Stop looking at women's magazines and call me in the morning."

CHAPTER 4

"What do you do?" This is the pervasive question at parties. But this question takes on a different meaning when you become a mother. As a cartoonist, I could stay home and change diapers while I changed pen nibs. But after childbirth, it is no longer about *you*. It's always about *them*. They own you, your body, and mind for a good 18 years.

I ended up having two beautiful daughters, which, frankly, terrified me. I was told girls are difficult, manipulative, and moody. The mother-daughter complex loomed over me each time the obstetrician said, "It's a girl!"

So what did I do? I baked cupcakes, wiped noses, joined the PTA and sewed strawberry costumes. Meanwhile, I got a contract at *The New Yorker*, authored seven children's books, wrote a history of the women cartoonists at *The New Yorker,* and compiled three cartoon collections. I even edited a collection of cartoons by women about mothers and daughters to help me understand what the heck I was going through.

Yes, my daughters had tantrums, but they never lived down to the reputation that girls have. They found their way into womanhood with ease, something that I was not so fortunate to experience. I like to think that all my "doing" was of some help.

HAIRSTYLES to AVOID in your 40s

You ask your Hair Stylist for something "New + Age Appropriate"

DISASTROUS!
1. She overestimated your age
2. She ignored you
3. She's making fun of you
4. She doesn't know the word "appropriate"
5. She hates her mother

Fixable with huge quantities of product

find a hat, scarf, or wig **NOW**

How to tell if he's cheating

Lipstick on his socks (and shirt and tie and pants and...)

He's spotted with...

He's extraordinarily helpful.

Does he act like Clinton, Spitzer, or Sanford?

You know your Sex Life is doomed when

He starts happily wearing bow ties and suspenders.

Comedy becomes more fun.

"I dreamt I was being cornered by giant wrinkles and tortured by menopause until a handsome plastic surgeon came and rescued me. What does it mean?"

Cleavage

Why do we bother?

too momish?

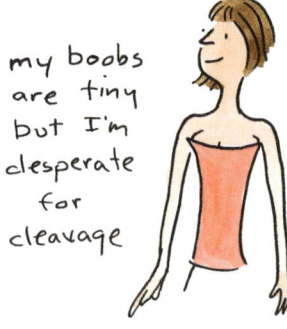

my boobs are tiny but I'm desperate for cleavage

high fashion or just really disturbing

show-off to annoy other women

LIPOSUCTION and YOU

Before you go under the vacuum, consider:

1. diet and exercise.

2. not looking so closely.

3. getting yelled at by loved ones who don't want you to do it.

4. Get a reality check.

GETTING AHEAD
Does it require:

1. plastic surgery

2. sexy suits

3. six-inch heels

4. loud voice

5. smarts

6. sharp elbows

7. cunning

8. cooking skills

GRAY HAIR

Many women never color their hair, so ease into, without confusion, being gray.

Some are lucky to have hair that grays interestingly.

But some women have NO IDEA what color their hair actually is, they've been coloring it for 30 years.

is it brown? blonde? green?

THE QUESTIONS ARE:

Am I ready to go gray?

Do my wrinkles and hair color go together?

Am I ready to don the ultimate symbol of "old"?

Do I look silly? Desperate?

(The worry will give you more gray!)

Don't get any edgier, Mom, or you'll fall off the edge.

"If I tell you your problem is old age, will you sue me?"

CHAPTER 5

50s

I always prided myself on the fact that I didn't buy a lot of face "product"—just soap. Then I turned 50. Strange little lines started to appear on my face. What *are* those? *Wrinkles*? I finally peered at the stuff in the cosmetic aisles at the drugstore—the area that looks vaguely like a doctor's office. I felt self-conscious. There were pots of things with names like: rejuvionolum method for early nighttime under-eye brightening and lifting, serumtology-inspired management system for total lip care, exfoliating system essentials for neck management during lunchtime. I purchased a $15, 1.5-ounce tube of eye cream and escaped unnoticed.

I spent a good part of my youth aware that I was being looked at—as a woman, and especially for my long blonde hair. I dressed for others: women, men, my grandmother, my editor, my deli owner—you name it. But in my 50s, I found myself in a new phase of always going unnoticed (except by my husband). This was something of a relief. Yet while this made me angry, it made me want to conform. And buy those $15 tiny tubes.

Maybe this was a small silver lining of going unnoticed—I could be content with how I looked because it wasn't really about what it used to be about. Now it was about what *I* wanted it to be about. Heck, no one will notice anyway.

You know you're getting older when

You think annual negative pap smear results are thrilling.

You don't care how cold the gynecological stirrups are.

You regularly and willingly submit to the smashing of your breasts in a machine.

You talk to complete strangers about hot flashes.

HAIRSTYLES to AVOID in your 50s

Reading glasses

(men <u>do</u> make passes at girls who wear glasses.)

Rebellious Body Parts

Does your upper arm have a mind of its own, dancing when there is no music?

Does your chin have no confidence, falling down on a daily basis?

Do your heels need a drink (more than you do)?

Things to Avoid when over 50

too much purple

too much scarf

too much hat

mirrors

low-rise, skinny jeans

brooches

house cleaning and cooking (haven't you done enough?)

one morning you woke up..

So you avoid mirrors and live in a fantasy world where you are still 26.

Top 10 Reasons to Lie About your Age

1. It's fun to fool people.
2. Your clothes aren't aging.
3. No one will notice anyway.
4. Your boyfriend is young.
5. Your boyfriend is old.
6. Your dog won't tell.
7. Age brings respect.
8. You loved being 52.
9. You're tired of being carded.
10. No one believes you're a grandmother.

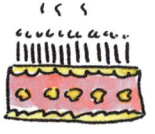

You're 50, you meet a 30-year-old guy. He's interested. You:

1. Hug him and don't let go

2. Run away

3. Tell him your inner mother is not available

4. Tell him your inner everything else is available

"I hear their marriage is in trouble."

CHAPTER 6

60s and beyond

I don't know if women in their 20s look at women in their 40s and think, that's what I want to be. I know I didn't. But now, in my 50s, my body is already telling me that I'm headed that way. One day, your knees are aching and wonder why: Oh, I am older, maybe *that's* why. In my mind, I'm 26, but my body tells me otherwise.

So I find myself seeking out women in their 60s and 70s, searching for role models. What part of me will sag? Will I wear long flowing gray hair, or short sassy white hair? I would like to look like Meryl Streep or Glenn Close—or even Whoopi Goldberg, but I think looking like her is a stretch. But I can model her attitude and spirit. You can't find that in a cream application. Growing up, the women I was fascinated with seemed to be full of life: my mother, Aunt Helen, my grandmother. They tried to be themselves in a world that often wouldn't let them. There weren't any women cartoonists to emulate, but two women writer friends of my family—Lucy Fletcher and Andy Logan—showed me that it was possible to be yourself creatively.

You don't need a mirror. I threw out the scale years ago, and now I want to toss the mirror. But I don't need to. Although it has taken me fifty years, I know who I am now, wrinkles and all. The mirror doesn't lie, but it can't tell me everything.

It seemed simple then, you were either/or. Now there are many ways to be older. Some of my favorites:

meryl Streep-type

whoopi Goldberg-girl

Hillary Clinton-cutie

Yoko Ono-cool

Susan Sarandon-Sultry

Rebellious Body Parts

Do your laugh lines want to stick around permanently?

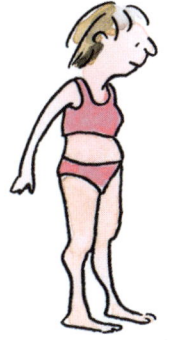

No matter how many crunches applied, your stomach muscles are staging a sit-down strike?

And remember that rear end you loved to hate? GONE.
(now you want it back, right?)

How **NOT** to get sucked into feeling old.

1. Don't take seat on bus.

2. Use memory loss as a tool.

3. Wear your reading glasses all the time during a bad date.

4. Get down on the floor with kids + dogs.

5. wake up happy.

6. Go skinny dipping.

7. Go with the flow.

8. throw out AARP mail.

9. Reward thoughtful youngsters.

At Heaven's Gate

He won't commit to leaving you alone.

or
to joining your feminist book group.

PERKS of OLD AGE

no period.

no stares from men.

getting waited on.

people listen.

Sagging Breasts

It's a slow descent.
One day, you realize that your beloved breasts are hanging out down with your navel.

What to do?

Lop them off and get new ones?

Camp out at Victoria's secret until you find the right one.

Throw away your bras and wear really baggy clothes. Pretend you don't care.

Put props under them.

Inflate them.

Sex in your 60s

It's all about slowly letting go.

say what you want:

do what you want:

about the author

Liza Donnelly is a staff cartoonist for *The New Yorker*. Her cartoons have appeared regularly since 1982, at which time she was the youngest cartoonist—and one of only three women cartoonists—at the magazine. She lives in New York with her husband, *New Yorker* cartoonist Michael Maslin, and their two daughters. See more of Liza's work at www.lizadonnelly.com.

If you have enjoyed this book
or it has touched your life in some way,
we would love to hear from you.

Please send your comments to:
Hallmark Book Feedback
P.O. Box 419034
Mail Drop 215
Kansas City, MO 64141

Or e-mail us at:
booknotes@hallmark.com